Exercise

By Tom Paxton   Illustrated by Don Vanderbeek

■■ ScottForesman

A Division of HarperCollins*Publishers*

Wiggle your fingers.

Bend your knees.

Touch your toes, now.

Lower please!

Stand on tiptoe.

Touch the skies.

It feels great to exercise!